Women
IN THE
ATHENIAN AGORA

SUSAN I. ROTROFF AND ROBERT D. LAMBERTON

AMERICAN SCHOOL OF CLASSICAL STUDIES AT ATHENS

2006

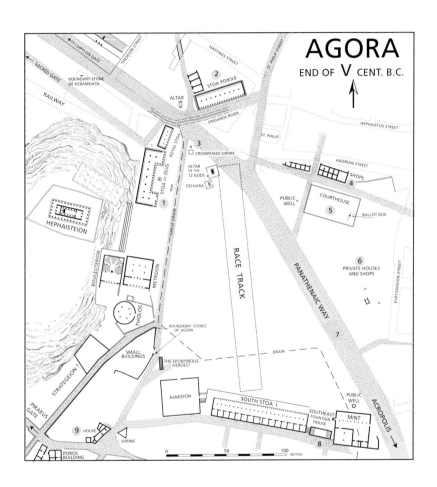

1. The Athenian Agora at the time Socrates and Ischomachos had their conversation. The Stoa of Zeus is at the upper left (1). Other places mentioned in this book are the Stoa Poikile (2), Crossroads Shrine (3), Courthouse (5), shops and houses just outside the agora (4, 6, 9), Panathenaic Way (7), and Southeast Fountain House (8).

INTRODUCTION

ONE DAY SOCRATES CAME UPON a prominent Athenian named Ischomachos sitting in the Stoa of Zeus in the Agora (1:1), waiting for some
men who were late for a meeting. Socrates remarked on Ischomachos's
uncharacteristic idleness, at odds with his reputation and stature in
the community. Ischomachos replied, "Well, Socrates, it's true I don't
spend my time at home—as far as the management of the household is
concerned my wife is certainly perfectly capable of looking after that."

When Socrates expressed interest in this arrangement, Ischomachos
gave an extensive account of the training and domestic responsibilities
of his wife. He recalled telling her when they married (he as an adult,
she at fourteen), that a certain division of activities was fundamental
to human affairs: "Since both our interests inside the household and
those outside demand their own specific activities and attention, I sup-
pose the gods fashioned human nature accordingly: the woman's for
the activities and business within the household, and the man's for the
activities and business outside."

This fictional account, from Xenophon's *Oikonomikos* or *Household
Management,* has done much to shape modern notions of how the classical Athenian household operated and of Athenian gender roles and
gender politics. If Xenophon's self-satisfied aristocrat were to be taken
at his word, the subject of women in the Agora would at best be an in-
teresting paradox. Backed by a chorus of other spokesmen of the Athenian patriarchy, he tells us quite emphatically that there *were no women*
(that is, no *respectable* women) in the Athenian Agora, that there *should*

2. THE SORT OF HOUSE ISCHOMACHOS'S WIFE MIGHT HAVE MANAGED: HOUSE OF THE GREEK MOSAIC (4TH CENTURY B.C.) NOT FAR FROM THE AGORA TO THE SOUTHWEST.

be no women in that most public of all public spaces. This was the arena of Athenian politics and business, of a civic order so dominated by male citizens of military age that the very voices of the city's other residents are drowned out by theirs. Public space, they insisted, was the property of male citizens: private space, the household, the place for women (2).

It is increasingly clear that this picture has more in it of wish-fulfillment than realistic depiction. In Xenophon's fiction, Socrates sits in an Agora devoid of women and engages a fellow citizen in discussion of this situation as if it were the natural order of the universe. If we could transport ourselves to the Stoa of Zeus in 410 B.C., however, the real-world spectacle around us would be quite different, and less strange and alienating than this fictional one. What follows is intended as a corrective to that ancient fiction, a portrait of an Agora in which women and women's concerns were present alongside men's, illustrated by evidence that excavations have unearthed concerning the lives of the women of classical Athens. Ancient images rarely come with explanatory labels, and thus they are often subject to differing interpretations. They do, however, counterbalance the circumscribed picture of women's activities that emerges from texts (authored by aristocratic men) with a richer, and perhaps more realistic, portrait of women's experience. Our concentration is on the Classical Agora of the 5th and 4th centuries B.C., with an epilogue on some of the modern women who were active in the recovery of that long-ago world.

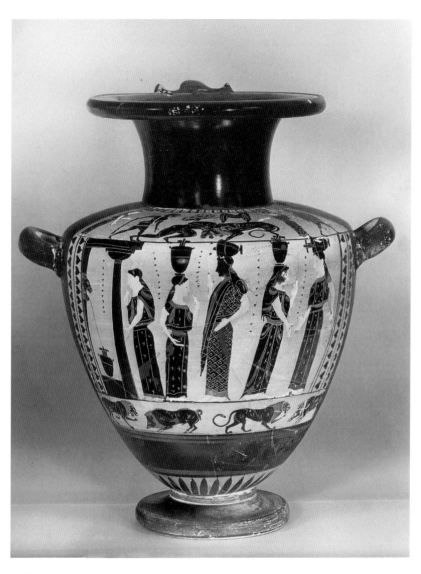

3. Women of Archaic Athens fetch water from a fountain house, on a water jug (hydria) of ca. 530 b.c. (Würzburg, Martin von Wagner Museum 304)

AT THE FOUNTAIN HOUSE

THE FIVE ELEGANTLY DRESSED WOMEN on an Attic water jug (hydria, 3) are visiting a fountain house, bringing empty pots of the same shape as the one that bears their portraits, filling them, and returning home. The scene might be the Southeast Fountain House in the Agora (1:8), but whichever fountain house it is, the message is clear: these women, finely turned out though they are, are performing a routine household task that takes them out of the house and into the public space of the city. They are hardly shielded from view. The painted inscriptions make the point as explicitly as one could wish: "Anthyle (Fleurette or Flora) is pretty," "Rhodon (Rosy) is pretty," "Hegesilla is pretty," and so on. Their clothing suggests that they are the daughters of well-to-do Athenians, though other interpretations of both their dress and their public visibility have been plausibly argued.

Whatever their status, these particular young women ran no risk of offending the notions of Socrates or Ischomachos concerning where women belonged. The pot was painted in the Athens of the tyrant Peisistratos, a generation before the traditional date of the establishment of Athenian democracy (508 B.C.) and over a century before the conversation imagined by Xenophon.

It seems likely that Archaic, aristocratic Athens, with its populist tyrants, was a less constrained environment for (at least some) Athenian women than the democratic Athens of the 5th and 4th centuries. Athenian democracy was, after all, a "one-weapon, one-vote" sort of democracy. The full participants were citizen males, whose claim to rule was founded on the fact that their military service, past or present, was the necessary condition for the survival—to say nothing of the lucrative imperialism—of Athens. The Archaic age evoked on the hydria, by contrast, was characterized by more blatant social stratification and by the economic and political dominance of a relatively small number of families. The women of these privileged families appear to have enjoyed greater freedom and greater access to public space than the women of 5th-century Athens, with its egalitarian ideology.

In Athens, as in most traditional societies, the work of the household fell largely to the women. It is not unlikely that, in the relatively simple economy of the Archaic period, the tasks that required going out in public were performed by the wives and daughters of the family—while, by contrast, in democratic 5th- and 4th-century Athens the shopping, the fetching of water, and so forth, were by preference assigned by the householders to slaves. They certainly talked that way, and we must admit that in the time of Perikles, Attic pots no longer offer these elegant scenes of women and girls at the fountain house.

A glimpse of the fountain house of the late 5th century, from Aristophanes' comedy *Lysistrata* (411 B.C.), shows how much the atmosphere had changed. The chorus of citizen women, explicitly described in the play as women who work (see p. 11) and thus not members of the leisure class, complain of the rowdy atmosphere at the spring:

> I barely managed to fill my hydria
> at dawn at the spring house—
> with the crowd and the noise and the clatter of pots,
> shoved around by slave-girls and scoundrels.

The gaiety evoked by the black-figure scene is gone; this sounds like a task that you would not undertake unless it were absolutely necessary. Those who could sent a slave. But slave or free, women were seen carrying those heavy pots across the Agora and through the streets of Athens. The one depicted here (4), full, would weigh about 16 kilos (35 pounds).

CLASSICAL WOMEN AND PUBLIC SPACE

LET US LISTEN TO ANOTHER of the voices that describe the gender politics of democratic Athens. His name was Euphiletos, and we know of him only from a law-court speech that he paid Lysias, one of the best of the Athenian professional speechwriters, to create for him. Accused of murder by the relatives of his victim, one Eratosthenes, his strategy is to admit the act and concentrate his defense on the circumstances. His story is that Eratosthenes seduced his wife, that he and a group of friends surprised the two together in the speaker's own bed, that Eratosthenes pleaded for his life, but the defendant dispatched him while spouting self-righteous claims to be acting on behalf of the state and the laws. That the laws of democratic Athens empowered such an offended husband to take the life of an adulterer is clear. Eratosthenes' relatives could only have alleged that the victim was entrapped or perhaps that the whole adultery story was a hoax to cover up some other hostile motive on the defendant's part. What interests us, in any case, is Euphiletos's presentation of himself to the jurors.

The accused portrays himself as a simple man whose great mistake in life was to trust his wife. He tried to keep an eye on her and to keep her away from temptation, but after a son was born he relaxed his vigilance. The crisis came at his mother's funeral, an apparently unavoidable exception to the rule that his wife remain in the women's quarters of his house, out of sight of males other than himself. At the funeral, Eratosthenes saw her and embarked on an ultimately successful seduction.

This text (known as *On the Murder of Eratosthenes* or simply Lysias 1) is roughly contemporary with Xenophon's *Household Management* and constitutes another of the prime exhibits for the case that Athenian citizen women were normally sequestered and kept invisible to males not of their household. Certainly, Euphiletos wants his jurors to view him as an outraged supporter of this notion, and he repeatedly invites those jurors to put themselves in his place so they may realize that he (and not the murdered man) is the offended party. Even if we factor in the situation that Euphiletos is on trial for his life, and presumably

5. SOME OF THE THINGS THAT WOMEN SOLD (P 10086, P 10118, P 10548)

willing to say anything he has to say to excuse his homicide, the shared values on which he builds both his case and his appeal to the jurors are nevertheless revealing. If we believe him, we would have to conclude that none of his jurors' wives ever appeared in public, much less in the Agora. Possibly they did not, but many other women did.

We often hear that an Athenian woman could not enter into contracts above a certain (low) value and that she had to be represented in larger transactions, or in court, by a male relative whom the law considered her *kyrios* (at best "guardian," at worst "lord and master"). In spite of these legal disabilities, however, Athenian women clearly did control property (see pp. 12–13) and also engaged in numerous professions, many of which took them into the public spaces of the city.

The Agora was the city's commercial hub; shops stood just outside its limits (1:4, 1:6), and hucksters set up temporary stalls inside its borders. In a system that seems odd to western shoppers, but prevails in many parts of the world, sellers of a single commodity were clumped together. Ischomachos, lecturing his wife on the importance of the orderly organization of the household, points out that the servants she sends to the Agora will know exactly where to go for each object or commodity. Fish sellers, for instance, congregated near the Stoa Poikile (1:2), chests were for sale near the law courts (1:5), perfume outside the Agora's southeast corner. A "women's agora" *(gynaikeia agora)* mentioned in 4th-century sources may have specialized in household goods or other items of particular interest to women.

It is to the comic plays of the 5th and 4th centuries, where we see an Athens closer to day-to-day reality than in other literary representations, that we must turn for sketches of the men and women who kept the shops. The plays provide abundant evidence for women as innkeepers and as merchants selling their wares in the market in the Agora. Aristophanes, for instance, invents two long compound words to describe the rank-and-file that Lysistrata marshals for her protest against the Peloponnesian War: seed-pulse-vegetable-women and garlic-innkeeper-bread-women. Women peddled salt, flour, honey, figs, fruits and vegetables (5), sesame, and clothing, and are particularly conspicuous as sellers of religious and luxury goods and items of personal adornment: incense, perfume (6), purple dye, wreaths, and ribbons. Whether they were slaves, metics (resident aliens), or citizens we do not know, but there was no lack of women merchants in the Agora.

Writers like Xenophon and Lysias would have us believe that citizen wives did not go to market. Euphiletos has a slave girl to do the shopping, so his wife can stay demurely in the women's quarters of the house. Ischomachos's wife manages the household from within. We may conclude that, compared to western markets today, more of the customers were men, and many of the female shoppers were slaves.

6. TWO WOMEN BARGAIN OVER PERFUMED OIL. THE SEATED SELLER HOLDS A PERFUME FLASK, WITH ANOTHER HANGING ON THE WALL BEHIND HER. (BERN, KUNSTHISTORISCHES MUSEUM 12227)

WOMEN AND PROPERTY

ATHENIAN LAW IS PECULIAR, from our perspective, in its emphasis on the nuclear, patriarchal household *(oikos),* often at the expense of the individual. Property was inherited through the male line, but the heir's right to dispose of that property was limited and his obligation to maintain its integrity enforceable by law. If, on the death of the head of a household, there was no male heir to succeed, then a daughter might become the provisional bearer of the property (as *epikleros,* misleadingly translated "heiress"), but she in effect became an adjunct to that property, and was married off to a close male relative of her father. A bride was likewise the bearer of property, sometimes considerable, from her father's *oikos* to that of her husband—her dowry—and although this property was attached to her and could not be claimed as his own by the husband except in extreme circumstances, the bride herself was generally unable to manage or dispose of it. The *epikleros* law, like the dowry legislation, provided for the material security of women without effectively putting any property in their control.

Here again, however, the apparent passivity and resourcelessness of Athenian women, implied (and perhaps envisioned) by the legal system, is at odds with much of the evidence of law-court speeches. That a woman might use the legal system to demand the rightful assignment of property is clear from Lysias's speech *Against Diogeiton,* where the widow of an Athenian named Diodotos (represented by her son-in-law as *kyrios*) sues her own father (who is also her brother-in-law) for abusing his own role as *kyrios* in order to defraud her children.

In the speech *Against Neaira* [Demosthenes], an unsympathetic prosecutor inadvertently created perhaps the most moving character in 4th-century Athenian literature. He narrates at length how Neaira, a Corinthian slave-prostitute, succeeded in buying her own freedom, escaping an abusive *kyrios,* establishing at law her right to some of the property she had taken with her, and, finally, living as the legitimate wife of a politically active Athenian citizen (the true target of the prosecution). This last act—the claim to be the legitimate wife of a citizen, whose children had the right to be treated as citizens—is the crime alleged.

7. Photograph and drawing of a mortgage inscription naming a woman. The first two letters of her name (ΔH) are preserved at the end of the second-to-last line. 4th or 3rd century b.c. (I 5639)

Neaira may have lost the case—we do not know the outcome—but the story of her victory, first over slavery and then over the legal disabilities she suffered in Athens as a woman and a foreigner, inevitably ennobles her in our eyes, while it both illuminates and indicts the gender politics of democratic Athens.

While Diodotos's widow enjoyed considerable privilege and exerted her influence within the system, though her canny move of using her son-in-law as *kyrios* against her father's claim to that role stretched the rules, Neaira is presented as a criminal. Her (retrospective) heroism lies in her defeating the system, at least for a time. If both managed in their different ways to take control of their lives and to exert their will over the disposition of property, there is little doubt that many other Athenian women defied the stereotype and did the same. Hard evidence comes from inscriptions, such as one carved on the boundary stone of a property in the residential neighborhood just to the south and west of the Agora (7). The house had been sold, but an outstanding loan prevented final transfer of title, and the stone was inscribed to bear witness to this state of affairs. What interests us is that the responsible party in the transaction (the *plerotria*, the initiator of the loan in question) is a woman, probably named Demo. Contrary to all expectation, she undertook this business without recourse to a *kyrios*.

8.

9.

10.

8. TWO WOMEN WITH A LOUTROPHOROS (CONTAINER FOR WATER FOR THE BRIDAL BATH) DECORATED WITH BRANCHES, PAINTED ON A LOUTROPHOROS OF CA. 400 B.C. (P 15139)

9. WOMEN PERFORMING A LINE-DANCE, MID-6TH CENTURY B.C. (PN-P 265)

10. EROS PRESENTS THE BRIDAL CROWN WHILE A WOMAN AND ANOTHER EROS BRING GIFTS; THE BRIDEGROOM LOOKS ON FROM THE SIDE. EARLY-4TH-CENTURY LEKANIS LID. (P 30350)

MARRIAGE AND WEDDINGS

Of all the occasions for a banquet, none is more conspicuous or talked about than a wedding—a wedding-feast advertises itself by the shouted marriage cry, the torch, and the double pipe; as Homer says, even the women stand in their doorways to watch and admire.

Plutarch, *Table Talk*

AS CONTRACTUAL ARRANGEMENTS BETWEEN HOUSEHOLDS *(oikoi),* Athenian marriages may not have been celebrations of true love consummated, but they were, nevertheless, celebrations. They were also occasions that brought women into public view, both as participants and audience. A procession of women brought water from a public fountain in a special pot—the loutrophoros—for the bridal bath (8). At the feast given by her *kyrios,* the bride's friends were at her side, they danced with her to celebrate the union (9), and they walked with her relatives in the bridal procession as she was taken to her husband's home.

Wedding scenes are frequently depicted on pots intended for women's use. The lid of a lekanis (10), a container for cosmetics and other toilet items, combines a scene showing the adornment of the bride (an Eros, the personification of desire, presents her with her bridal crown) with the gift giving *(epaulia)* that took place on the day after the wedding feast. On a smaller cosmetic and jewelry container (11), the bride, bowing her head with appropriate modesty, is followed by another woman who holds three stacked libation bowls, probably part of the equipment she is taking to her new home. The bride's friends and female relatives carry chests on their heads, gifts for the bride or perhaps her trousseau, in a wedding procession on a black-figure lebes, a basin used in the nuptial bath (12); the stand below depicts her future duties. On the wall of another such basin (13) the bride fingers her garment nervously as she bends her head to be crowned by an Eros (almost completely lost). The brides often look subdued, perhaps even a little anxious; after all, they are leaving their familiar homes for a future with an unknown bridegroom. Who knows if he will be a sympathetic partner or not?

11.

13.   12.

11. A MODEST BRIDE, ON A COSMETIC CONTAINER OF CA. 430–420 B.C. (P 6980)

12. NUPTIAL BASIN ON A STAND: THE WEDDING PROCESSION ABOVE, WOOL-WORKING BELOW. LATE 6TH CENTURY B.C. (P 7893, P 7897)

13. EROS CROWNS THE BRIDE ON A NUPTIAL BASIN OF CA. 420 B.C. (PN-P 48)

DIVORCE

MARRIAGES COULD BE DISSOLVED RELATIVELY easily in classical Athens, but the details of the procedure and the true dynamics of such actions elude us. The dowry, in any case, was crucial. If an Athenian rejected his wife, she reverted to the charge of her previous *kyrios* (her father, if he was still living), and her dowry went with her. Conversely, an abused or otherwise unhappy wife might prefer to return (with her dowry) to her father's *oikos* and might enlist his help in doing so. In both instances, the prospect of the loss of the dowry may be assumed to have offered some protection to women by exerting a moderating influence on a husband inclined either to maltreatment or to rejection.

Various less familiar factors were also involved. For instance, the death, without male issue, of the father of a married woman could result in the annulment of her marriage to free her to marry one of her father's relatives, in the name of the preservation of the *oikos*. Instances of this practice are invoked in law-court speeches involving inheritances, and the playwrights of the romantic Athenian New Comedy of the 4th century built plots around the threat to the aspirations of young lovers represented by the claims on a young heiress *(epikleros)* of elderly (and decidedly romantically unattractive) relatives.

Divorces were, in practice, almost exclusively initiated by males—whether by the husband in rejecting a wife, or by the wife's relatives, either on their own or at the instigation of the wife who wanted to escape a marriage that was distasteful to her. One feisty woman of the 5th century, Hipparete, tried to take affairs into her own hands (**14**). Disgusted by the flagrant philandering of her husband, the brilliant but erratic general Alcibiades, she left him and returned to the home of her brother. When this had no effect on her husband's behavior, she went on her own to the office of the magistrate to record a divorce. It did her no good; Alcibiades

14. A WOMAN FROM THE TIME OF HIPPARETE, CA. 430–420 B.C. (P 5865)

apprehended her and dragged her very publicly through the Agora and back home. But she made gossip headlines; the story was still considered worth repeating over five centuries later, when Plutarch composed his biography of Alcibiades.

RITUAL

THE ATHENIAN CALENDAR BRISTLED WITH religious festivals, and their observance played a large part in the life of the populace. The significance of these occasions was especially great in the case of women, since they provided a reason to leave the home and mingle with people outside the immediate family.

Many religious duties could be performed only by women. The cults of female divinities, for instance, were normally overseen by women. Thus, a priestess officiated in the worship of Athena, the patron divinity and namesake of the city (15). She was normally chosen from members of the clan of the Eteoboutadai, aristocrats who claimed descent from Boötes, brother of the legendary first king of Athens. Although the overall organization of Athena's major festival was in the hands of the magistrates (all male, of course), the priestess officiated at sacrifices and was a person of some influence. Herodotos tells us (8.41), for instance, that her report that the sacred snake, guardian of Athena's temple on the Acropolis, had ceased to eat the honey cake that was offered to it monthly supported the Athenians' decision to abandon their city to the invading Persians in 480 B.C.

15. ATHENA, PATRON GODDESS OF ATHENS, CA. 410 B.C. (P 14793)

Such positions and honors were restricted to the elite few. The women of the chorus of Aristophanes' *Lysistrata* establish their social status by listing the religious duties they performed as girls:

> As soon as I turned seven I was an *arrephoros,*
> Then at ten I was *aletris* for the goddess;
> Then, shedding my yellow robe, I was a bear at the Brauronia;
> and once, as a lovely young girl, I was a *kanephoros.*

The *arrephoroi* were entrusted with the transfer of secret objects between the Acropolis and the lower city; they spent a year of their girlhood living on the Acropolis (where they were provided with a playground for ball games) and also wove the first threads of the sacred robe (peplos) presented to Athena at her festival (see pp. 34–36). The *aletris* ground grain for the preparation of sacred cakes.

These honors were the perquisites of the daughters of aristocratic families, but a larger number of Athenian girls took part in the third rite, the *Arkteia,* or bear-festival, in honor of Artemis. Since Artemis was the goddess concerned with childbirth, the most perilous experience of an ancient woman's life, her goodwill was especially important for those approaching the end of their girlhood. Initiation involved a period of residence in the goddess's sanctuary at Brauron, in the eastern part of the Attic countryside. We do not know the details of the ceremony, but races and dances made up part of it. These are shown on a series of small kraters (wine-mixing bowls) that have been found in sanctuaries of Artemis all over Attica and that were probably used in the course of this ritual. Some have turned up in the Agora; possibly they once stood as equipment or dedications in the shrine of Artemis on the Acropolis. A fragment of one (16) shows the girls clothed and dancing hand in hand; other kraters show them nude and competing in races.

16. ATHENIAN GIRLS PERFORMING THE BEAR DANCE, WHILE A GOAT JOINS IN AT THE LEFT. LATE 5TH CENTURY B.C. (P 27342)

As the culmination of her girlhood, an aristocratic young woman might serve as a *kanephoros* in one of the major civic festivals. Her duty was to carry the kanoun, a basket containing barley and a knife, basic equipment for the sacrifice that formed the centerpiece of Greek religious practice. *Kanephoroi* were virgins on the threshold of marriage, therefore probably in their early teens. As many as a hundred walked each summer in the Panathenaic procession, in honor of Athena, the route of which took them through the middle of the Agora (**1:7**). Other female participants in this parade were the priestess of Athena, as well as metic (non-citizen) women who carried water jars, stools, and parasols. As we have seen, women traditionally carried burdens on their heads; a terracotta figurine (**17**) shows a young woman carrying an elaborate kanoun, perhaps made of metal and decorated with the image of a divinity.

17. WOMAN CARRYING A KANOUN, 4TH CENTURY B.C. (T 104)

18. NORTHWEST CORNER OF THE AGORA IN THE LATE 5TH CENTURY; THE CROSSROADS SHRINE IS IN THE FOREGROUND.

Women of all classes could also be seen making offerings at the small shrines that dotted the Agora. At the northern side of the square, where the Panathenaic Way joins the road along the west side of the Agora, is a small square enclosure (1:3, 18). Clearly a shrine, it encompasses an unusual outcropping of limestone—a sort of natural altar—and in the latter part of the 5th century people threw hundreds of votive gifts into the little precinct (19). We do not know who was worshipped here (hence the descriptive label: Crossroads Shrine), but the nature of the votive gifts tells us that the shrine was particularly frequented by women: hundreds of perfume flasks of various shapes, jewelry, gilded pebbles, baby feeders, loom weights and spindle whorls, along with vessels decorated with intimate scenes of women's activities (20). Their presence in the Crossroads Shrine bears witness to the presence of the donors—women—in the Agora.

Women also set up more substantial memorials to their piety, like the relief plaque (21) dedicated to a nameless hero by a woman named Chrysis; it probably once stood in one of the many small

19. SMASHED POTTERY ON AND AROUND THE ROCK IN THE SHRINE

20. VOTIVE GIFTS OF THE SORT DEDICATED IN THE CROSSROADS SHRINE (P 10282, P 29369, P 29544, P 29662)

21. Dedication of Chrysis to a hero (I 4707)

shrines in and around the Agora. At the left, Chrysis and a smaller figure, her daughter or possibly her servant, approach the larger-than-life hero and his female companion.

THE DANCE OF THE MAENADS

> To dance for joy in the forest,
> to dance where the darkness is deepest
> where no man is . . .
>
> Euripides, *Bacchai*

GREEK LITERATURE IS RICH IN FANTASIES of a world without women; the chorus of Euripides' *Bacchai* (performed in 406 B.C.) goes in search of a world at least provisionally without men. In the play, the women of Thebes have left their homes to participate in the wild rites of Dionysos, god of wine and intoxication. They dance on the mountain, pursuing animals and tearing them apart in the brutal rite called *sparagmos*. It all ends badly, as the queen's son becomes their victim, a punishment for his opposition to the Bacchic rites.

The *Bacchai* dramatizes the events of Greek mythology, but bacchai (devotees of Bacchos, another name for Dionysos) and maenads (raving women) were also a part of the real world, as participants in the ecstatic

22. MAENAD WITH THYRSOS, 510–500 B.C. (P 24116)

worship of Dionysos at cities throughout Greece. Every other year, probably in mid-winter, Athenian women joined women from Delphi in a dance on the heights of Mount Parnassos. This was a strenuous activity, and not without its dangers. One year a blizzard overtook the dancers and rescue parties had to be sent out. Another time the women became lost in the dark and wandered into a neighboring town, collapsing into an exhausted sleep in the public marketplace. In a moving show of gender solidarity, women of the town kept watch, protecting the maenads as they slept, offered them assistance and food when they awoke, and accompanied them to the border on their homeward journey.

Images of maenads are common on Greek pottery, but in both literature and art it is difficult to disentangle myth from reality. Euripides' account insists, however, that this was no drunken orgy: his bacchai are not intoxicated (they drink milk, not wine) but rather possessed by the god, and despite the erotically charged atmosphere of some of the vase paintings, sexual license is not a part of the rite that Euripides describes.

The images leave us in no doubt about the appearance of the maenads. They wield the thyrsos, a long staff made of the light stem of a giant fennel plant bound with a bunch of ivy leaves at one end (**22–23, 27**).

23. MAENADS DANCING. THE WOMAN AT LEFT BEATS THE TYMPANON, THE ONE AT RIGHT CARRIES A THYRSOS, 420–410 B.C. (P 12632)

24. (LEFT) Dancing maenad playing a krotalon, with satyr at right, on a drinking cup of ca. 500 b.c. (P 8709)

25. (RIGHT) Dionysos crowned with ivy and carrying his signature wine cup, ca. 500 b.c. (P 12236)

Sometimes they carry small animals, snakes twine around their arms, and they throw back their heads in song; but chiefly they dance, to the music of the double pipe, the krotalon (a percussion instrument, like an oversized castanet, **24**), and the tympanon (drum, **23**). They may be accompanied by Dionysos himself (**25**), or by satyrs, lusty fertility spirits with equine features (pointed ears and long tails, **24**, **26**); whether

26. Pairs of maenads and satyrs dance on a drinking cup of the third quarter of the 6th century b.c. (P 1241)

these are imagined, divine companions, or masked male participants we do not know. The maenads also take part in more conventional ritual (27), but a libation may be a prelude to more exotic activities.

The Bacchic rites present a striking departure from the usual roles of Athenian women. No longer homebodies attending to children and weaving, they throw off conventions utterly, gathering together out of doors, far from home, and without the male supervision that hemmed in almost every other aspect of their lives.

27. MAENAD WITH THYRSOS POURS A LIBATION ONTO AN ALTAR, 430–420 B.C. (P 5262)

FUNERALS

THE SELF-SERVING AND SELF-PITYING Euphiletos (p. 9) has lent an exaggerated prominence to the funeral among the occasions on which the respectable Athenian matron escaped the women's quarters of her home to be seen in public. His wife's exposure to the desirous glances of Eratosthenes at the funeral of his mother was the prelude to her downfall.

The procession from home to burial place was not the only aspect of the care of the dead in which women figured prominently. It would normally fall to the women of the house to tend the corpse from the moment of death, as mourners, as bathers, and as dressers. In this last capacity, they wrapped the corpse in the shroud they had in most cases woven.

In the repertory of Athenian potters, the white-ground lekythos (a container for perfumed oil) is the shape with the strongest associations with death and funerals. Their decoration is exceptionally vivid,

applied as it is to a white background (otherwise quite rare in Greek figured vases). The scenes are often funereal. A disproportionate number of lekythoi are preserved intact, because they were deposited in the tomb at the end of the ceremonies.

On the lekythos illustrated here (28; its decoration "rolled out" and enlarged below), a woman visits a grave monument of unusual, ovoid shape. It is festooned with an abundance of ribbons from the funeral that has just occurred. She holds an alabastron from which she is about to pour a libation of perfumed oil in commemoration of the deceased, a young man who lurks, heavily cloaked, beside his grave.

28. White-ground lekythos (oil flask) from a 5th-century cemetery outside the city, found in a rescue excavation supervised by Virginia Grace (see pp. 49–50) in 1936 (P 10277)

AT HOME: THE WOMEN'S WORLD

THE AGORA EXCAVATIONS HAVE CONCERNED themselves primarily with public space, but the limits of the Athenian Agora evolved over time and private houses always lay just beyond them. Thus houses of all periods have come to light in the excavations (1:6, 1:9), and within their walls, it was the women of Athens who were largely in control.

In the following sections, we will take a look at some of the characteristic and well-documented activities of women within Athenian households, as well as the evidence for how that space was organized and partitioned (if indeed it was partitioned) for the particular use of women and men. Written accounts are few, because Athenian literature does not open the doors of contemporary private life to allow us to peer inside. Painted pottery, like the clearly private scene at right (29), and the houses themselves, however, provide good clues to the reconstruction of that private world.

29. TWO WOMEN ON A LEKANIS LID OF THE SECOND QUARTER OF THE 4TH CENTURY B.C.; PERHAPS A SCENE OF DRESSING THE BRIDE FOR HER WEDDING. (PN-P 110)

IN THE GYNAIKONITIS

THE GENDER-BASED PARTITIONING OF Athenian space into public/male and private/female has proven less clear-cut in reality than Ischomachos and Euphiletos, as the outspoken proponents of the democratic Athenian ideology, would have us believe. But what about the allocation of space within the home? Did the women of the household have the run of the whole establishment, or were they sequestered in the areas where fabric and perhaps food preparation took place, protected from the eyes and the attentions of men from outside the household? Once again, we have literary evidence for rigorous segregation, while the evidence of archaeology and of 4th-century comedy seems to point to a more fluid and permeable allocation of space.

The "women's quarters" of a dwelling—whether the seraglio of an eastern potentate or the bedroom and related space of an Athenian housewife—were called in Greek a *gynaikon* or *gynaikonitis*. This latter term in fact enters the literature with Lysias's client Euphiletos and Xenophon's Ischomachos.

In Euphiletos's modest house (as he insists with a warmth that may raise our suspicions) the distinction was rigid and proper. The women lived upstairs, away from the street door and from the semipublic space where Euphiletos himself might entertain his friends. Those arrangements were changed for his wife's convenience, while she was nursing, leading to the events described on page 9. Ischomachos's house was much grander than that of Euphiletos, and its men's quarters were separated from the *gynaikonitis* by a bolted door. Ischomachos insists on this detail to underline the importance of keeping male and female slaves segregated, in order to set limits on their erotic activity and their pilfering. What, if any, impact this segregation might have had on his own wife's comings and goings is unclear.

Archaeology is unlikely to help us very much here, since the second stories of ancient houses (perhaps the most likely location for a truly segregated *gynaikonitis*) are virtually never preserved. Hellenistic houses on the island of Delos and 4th-century ones at sites such as Priene and Olynthos, where domestic architecture is far better preserved than in Athens, show no trace of apartments or rooms segregated for women's use. In the romantic New Comedy of 4th-century Athens, enjoyed, translated, and adapted by the Romans, there survive several references to "women's quarters," enabling us to say at least that certain parts of a 4th-century house were likely to be the special preserve of the women of the household. In these plays, however, that rigorous domestic segregation of the sexes is generally marked as old-fashioned and severe (and hence, everything that New Comedy rejects).

The very centrality of weaving to the traditional picture of women's domestic activities is also suggestive. Weaving requires light, usually sunlight, and sunlight was available in Athenian houses principally in and around the central courtyard. There is every reason to believe that looms were set up in such places, quite accessible to the street, and that they could be moved around for the convenience of the weavers.

All of this suggests a partition of space that was flexible, and that may have been quite different at ten in the morning and ten at night. The ground-floor courtyard, giving access to the asymmetrical dining area traditionally identified by archaeologists as the *andron* or men's dining room (30), may well have been the scene of women's activities by day, though women would have avoided it when the head of the household was entertaining his friends.

Even if Euphiletos and Ischomachos paint a picture of living arrangements not dissimilar to those in a traditional Islamic house, with rigorously segregated space for men and for women, Athenian houses are more likely to have been characterized by a greater openness and flexibility in the use of space by the men and women of the household.

All this being said, numerous scenes on Greek vases of an intimate world where women dress, adorn themselves, and pass whatever leisure

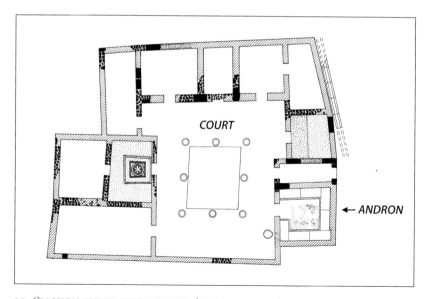

30. CLASSICAL HOUSE SOUTH OF THE AGORA

31. (TOP) DRESSING SCENE ON A WATER JUG OF CA. 430 B.C. A WOMAN HOLDS THE OVERFOLD OF HER GARMENT IN HER MOUTH AS SHE KNOTS HER BELT. ANOTHER WOMAN BRINGS THE CLOAK THAT WILL COMPLETE HER ENSEMBLE. (P 6053)

32. (BOTTOM) THE LADY OF THE HOUSE HOLDS A PERFUME FLASK AND A FLOWER; A COMPANION OR SERVANT STANDS BESIDE THE BED AT THE LEFT. A FINELY DECORATED EPINETRON, CA. 440–430 B.C. (P 18283)

they could snatch from their household tasks, are as close as we are likely to get to a peek into the *gynaikonitis*. The vases preserve fascinating details of ordinary life, such as the technique women normally used for tying the belt below the overfold of a garment (31). These activities take place in a room furnished with a couch and an elegant chair, in which the lady of the house sits while companions or servants present her with perfume or jewelry (32), or she passes the time with a game. Other furnishings would have included the chests (illustrated in 34) that held her wardrobe and other textiles, the fruit of her labors with the spindle and the loom. There must also have been a table on which she could range her toiletries—perfume flasks (33) and containers for her jewelry and makeup (34). Fragments of the containers are frequently found in the wells and cisterns that served the houses located around the Agora. Jewelry is much less common, for any woman who lost an earring such as those illustrated in 35 would certainly have searched hard until she found it. As luck would have it, however, one of these was dropped down a well (possibly as a votive gift), and the other was found along the side of the Panathenaic Way.

33. Perfume flasks, 5th and 4th centuries b.c. (P 15211, P 24551, P 28679)

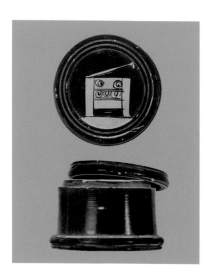

34. (left) Cosmetic box with picture of a chest on its lid, late 5th century b.c. (P 23897)

35. (right) Gold earrings: youthful Eros with a ribbon (4th century b.c.), baby Eros playing the kithara (Hellenistic). (J 154, J 160)

TEXTILES

THE PRINCIPAL DOMESTIC TASK OF Greek women—beyond reproduction—was the manufacture of cloth and clothing for their families. Athenian girls and women spent much—perhaps most—of their time engaged in this activity. It was not quite a feminine monopoly, for male weavers are attested in the literary sources, but the working of wool, and especially the laborious tasks of cleaning, combing, and spinning, seem to have been almost exclusively in the hands of women. They worked wool at home to provide cloth for household needs, and some women were also employed in this capacity in weaving establishments. Freedwomen (former slaves) are attested as working in this profession by numerous Attic inscriptions.

The Greek household aimed at self-sufficiency, and in the sphere of clothing it was actually possible to attain that elusive goal. Wool was the commonest textile; a small family flock supplied the raw material, which was then processed by the women of the household, with the assistance of slaves if the family was sufficiently well-off. Almost all of the textiles themselves have perished, but some of the tools for their manufacture survive along with ancient descriptions and depictions of the wool-working process (36–41).

In Aristophanes' *Lysistrata,* the protagonist suggests the application of the wool-working process to politics. In doing so she gives a vivid picture of the operation:

> Plunge it in a basin to wash out the filth.
> Lay it on a bench and beat out the burrs—and evildoers.
> Comb out conspirators, pluck out the pills.
> Gather together friends, residents, foreigners,
> debtors, and those in our overseas colonies.
> Comb into a basket of common good will.
> Winding all these in a big ball of yarn,
> weave a great cloak for The People.

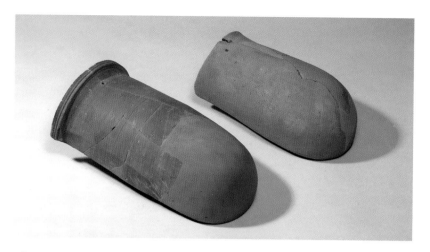

36. PLACED OVER THE KNEE, AN EPINETRON PROVIDED A FIRM SURFACE FOR WORK-
ING WOOL. THESE TWO EXAMPLES DATE IN THE LAST QUARTER OF THE 5TH CENTURY
B.C. (P 9445, P 18605)

37. SPINDLE WHORLS, 6TH
AND EARLY 5TH CENTURIES
B.C. (MC 365, MC 373, MC
938, MC 948)

38. WOMEN WORK WOOL
ON A STAND FOR A NUPTIAL
BASIN OF THE LATE 6TH CEN-
TURY B.C. (SEE 12). A WOOL
BASKET SITS ON THE FLOOR
BETWEEN THEM. (P 7897)

39. WOMAN WITH WOOL
BASKET, 460–450 B.C.
(P 30068)

The wool is washed to clean away grease and dung, beaten to remove debris, and then combed and worked into large sausage-shaped rolls. These might be formed by rolling and twisting the wool over the thigh, in which case an epinetron (32, 36) could be used for comfort and to provide a firmer surface. The wool was then weighed and placed in a kalathos, a distinctive flaring basket; it is this activity that engages the women on the stand for a nuptial lebes (38), working in pairs to make the task go more quickly. The wool was now ready for spinning, a task performed with a distaff and a drop spindle; the woman on a red-figure lekythos (39) may be spinning, with her wool basket in front of her. The spindle was wooden, but a pierced clay weight—a spindle whorl—was placed over its tip to give it momentum as it spun. Many of these have survived, some nicely glazed and decorated (37).

The cloth was woven on an upright loom, the warp weighted by clay loom weights (40, 41). These too survive in large numbers and in a variety of shapes: pyramidal, discoid, and biconical. While most are undecorated, some are glazed or carry little stamps, perhaps designed to identify them as part of a set.

All of this took a good deal of time. It is estimated that, working fairly consistently at her task, a woman would need a month to prepare the wool, about a week to set up her loom, and then a few days to weave a simple woolen garment. Much cloth, however, was anything but simple. Although true tapestry could not be produced on the Greek loom, other weaving techniques, together with embroidery, were used to decorate cloth. The results are best known from vase paintings (42, 43).

Girls learned these skills young. Ischomachos tells Socrates that when he brought home his fourteen-year-old wife, she knew how to work wool, make clothes, and supervise the spinning done by the women slaves. Girls aged between seven and eleven were entrusted with the

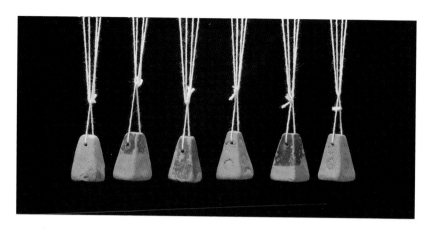

40. LOOM WEIGHTS (MC 867, MC 1129, MC 1193, MC 1230, MC 1499, MC 1502)

41. WOMEN WEAVING ON AN UPRIGHT LOOM, THE WARP THREADS WEIGHTED WITH LOOM WEIGHTS BELOW. THE WOMAN ON THE LEFT BEATS THE LAST-WOVEN WEFT THREAD AGAINST THE TEXTILE AT THE TOP; THE WOMAN ON THE RIGHT PREPARES TO WEAVE THE NEXT WEFT THREAD. THE SHUTTLE, WRAPPED WITH YARN, RESTS WEDGED BETWEEN THE WARP THREADS AT THE LEVEL OF THE CROSSBAR; OTHER SHUTTLES ARE PLACED AT THE LEFT AND THE RIGHT ENDS OF THE BAR. MID-6TH CENTURY B.C. (METROPOLITAN MUSEUM OF ART, FLETCHER FUND 1931 [31.11.10]).

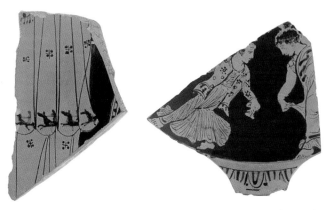

42. (LEFT) WOMEN'S WORK: PATTERNED GARMENT, 470–460 B.C. (P 9757)

43. (RIGHT) DANCING WOMEN ON THE LID OF A CONTAINER FOR COSMETICS OR JEWELRY, CA. 420–410 B.C. ONE WOMAN WEARS A PATTERNED JACKET AND CARRIES A KROTALON; THE OTHER WEARS A MANTLE WITH A PATTERNED BORDER. (PN-P 96)

beginning of the weaving of one of the most famous of Athenian textiles, the peplos (robe) for the ancient and holy statue of Athena on the Acropolis. This was an elaborate, patterned cloth, the design of which traditionally included a representation of the battle between the gods and the giants. It took nine months to complete it, and many women participated in its creation. In the Hellenistic period they were even honored on inscriptions, one of the few instances in which women's names were displayed in a public place.

HOUSEHOLD RESPONSIBILITIES

THE MANUFACTURE AND PROCESSING OF fabric are the best documented of the household activities of Athenian women, but writers like Xenophon and Lysias point to further and far-reaching responsibilities. Lysias's client Euphiletos and Xenophon's Ischomachos each claim to have turned the running of their households over to their wives. This seems in practice to have meant supervising various slaves, and the complex-

44. STORAGE BINS, 5TH TO 3RD CENTURIES B.C. (P 3563, P 9630, P 23681)

ity of the task would have varied widely according to the wealth of the household. Euphiletos's wife had only a single slave girl to do household work and errands, but Ischomachos's wife was encouraged to learn to supervise the girl who did the baking as well as the "housekeeper" *(tamia)*. Most housewives, though, must have been their own housekeepers, taking personal responsibility for, and authority over, the stores of foodstuffs and other goods essential to the running of the household—goods that were stored in large clay jars (44), in rooms that could be secured with a lock (45).

45. BRONZE LOCK PLATE FROM A HOUSE DESTROYED BY THE PERSIANS IN 480 B.C. (B 1335)

CHILD CARE

THERE HAVE BEEN FEW SOCIETIES in which men have shouldered much of the drudgery of child care and ancient Athens was in this area quite unexceptional; child care was emphatically women's work. Young women are shown bouncing children on their knees (46), and it was common for new brides to handle babies—a practice that, it was thought, enhanced their chances of producing offspring of their own (47). Once a baby arrived, families who could afford it might hire a wet-nurse to relieve the mother of the demanding task of suckling the infant. Soranos, a medical writer of the 2nd century A.D., gives a cut-and-dried set of instructions for what to look for when selecting such a retainer: "choose a woman not younger than 20, not older than 40, who has given birth two or three times, healthy, in good condition, large and with a good color, with breasts of medium size" (Soranos naturally has a good deal more to say about the breasts). The woman should be "modest, sympathetic, even-tempered, Greek, and clean." Such a person will be able not only to nourish and safeguard the child, but also to ensure that its first lisped syllables will be in proper Greek.

46. (LEFT) MULTITASKING: A YOUNG WOMAN AND A CHILD, WITH A WOOL BASKET AT RIGHT, CA. 510–500 B.C. (P 13363)

47. (RIGHT) BABY BOY ON A MINIATURE JUG, CA. 420 B.C. (P 21227)

48. Terracotta figurine, ca. 200 b.c. (PN-T 114)

Many of the caregivers for the young, however, were elderly women, whether slave or free, like the old woman who kisses a baby here (48). The headless, ageless nurse of the other terracotta (49), however, who comforts a toddler we might imagine to be either screaming or simply shy, represents in more general terms this everyday reality of a considerable portion of the human race. There is evidence that their nurturing efforts did not go unappreciated. Some time after the middle of the 4th century b.c. a well-to-do woman composed or commissioned a poem to be inscribed as an epitaph on the tombstone of her nurse, a metic woman named Melitte.

49. Nurse and her charge. Terracotta figurine, 4th century b.c. (T 214)

Here beneath the earth lies the nurse
of Hippostrate—and she misses you:
"Nurse, while you lived I loved you, and now
I still honor you though departed, and will do so
as long as I live. If the good are rewarded,
I know you have your reward,
and that for you, before all others, honors await
in the house of Persephone and Pluto."

(*IG* II² 7873)

COMPANIONS

NEAIRA'S PROSECUTOR (see pp. 12–13) offers this succinct set of definitions in order to show how she has violated accepted social roles: "We have companions (hetairai) for pleasure, concubines for the day-to-day service of our bodies, and wives to bear us legitimate children and faithfully watch over our household goods." In a society where men traditionally married late and extramarital relationships with women of citizen status were very dangerous, prostitution flourished. A comic play attributes the official establishment of brothels throughout the city to the legendary Athenian lawmaker Solon (ca. 600)—though it scarcely seems possible that they were absent earlier. In any event, encounters between prostitutes and the men of Athens are a common topic of vase painting. Courtship as we know it did not exist between young men and respectable women; the youth below (50) offers his gift to a woman whose company is for hire.

Prostitution was a legal activity, sanctioned, licensed—and taxed— by the state. Prostitutes might be slaves or freeborn, though women of citizen status are virtually unattested in the profession. Some prostitutes who were born into slavery managed to buy their freedom, but they might well continue to ply their trade; without significant capital or legal rights, they had little alternative. If they were highly successful, they might train others in their craft and themselves maintain a brothel.

At the top of the scale were the hetairai, or "companions," women who not only provided the usual sexual services but had other talents as well. They knew how to play a musical instrument, perhaps, or to sing and to dance. Aspasia,

50. A YOUTH OFFERS A GIFT (EGG? FRUIT?) TO A WOMAN, 470–460 B.C. (P 30056)

a hetaira who lived for over a decade with the powerful 5th-century politician Perikles, is reputed to have been proficient in the (normally manly) art of rhetoric. Some hetairai, like Phryne, are said to have been strikingly beautiful; two different 4th-century artists were so taken with her that they used her as the model for images of Aphrodite, the goddess of love. While such anecdotes may be fictional, they reflect the range of admiration successful professionals might evoke. The apparent freedom of these women may have a certain appeal to the modern observer, especially in comparison to the more circumscribed lives of citizen women. Most women who lived from the sale of their bodies, however, led far less glamorous lives, with their incomes and their choices diminishing as they grew older. Artists might admire the great beauties at their prime, but the

51. HETAIRA RECLINING WITH A CUSTOMER AT A SYMPOSIUM, CA. 430 B.C. (P 5694+20043)

52. RECLINING HETAIRA WITH KROTALON, 520–510 B.C. (P 23133)

aging prostitute, her wrinkles thinly disguised by rouge and paint, is the butt of many jokes on the Athenian comic stage. Existence outside the boundaries of conventional society was not easy for anyone, but least of all for women.

Athenian men left their wives behind when they met for the symposium—the drinking bout that was the extension of an aristocratic dinner. The entertainment featured songs and games, along with sexual play. Hetairai were often present, and they are frequently pictured on the drinking cups that circulated at those gatherings. Sometimes they recline with the men (51; only a trace of the garment of the man to the right is preserved), or play a musical instrument (52, where a nude reclining hetaira holds a krotalon). After the drinking the party-makers

53. An exotic blond flute-girl accompanies men on a revel. The man behind her carries a jar full of wine, ca. 500 b.c. (P 1544)

frequently took to the streets in the *komos,* a drunken revel; a flute-girl accompanies them as musician on a black-figure drinking cup (53)—another woman walking through the public streets of Athens. Flute-girls were paid to provide musical entertainment (and the fee they could charge was fixed by law), but they were doubtless called upon for sexual favors as well.

Vase painters, decorating the drinking cups that were used at the symposium, sometimes give us imagined pictures of hetairai in the privacy of their own homes. Their nudity and their exotic accessories assure us that these are not Athenian matrons, and their beauty and luxurious surroundings indicate that they functioned at the high end of their profession. In a scene painted on the floor of a late-6th-century drinking cup (54), a woman, naked except for a large earring and an elaborately wrapped kerchief, offers a wreath at a flaming altar, located in the courtyard of her house; she might be propitiating Aphrodite Hetaira, patroness of prostitutes. Another (55), similarly ornamented, has perhaps just finished her bath in the basin that sits at the bottom of the picture, and prepares to don an elegant pair of soft boots. The

IMAGES ON THE FLOORS OF LATE-
6TH-CENTURY DRINKING CUPS.

Clockwise from top left:

54. HETAIRA OFFERING A WREATH
AT AN ALTAR (P 24102)

55. BATHING HETAIRA (P 24131)

56. A WOMAN AWAITS HER BED-
MATE (P 2574)

status of the woman on another cup (56) is more ambiguous. She gazes into a mirror, checking her appearance as she awaits the person who will share the couch pictured at the right; but is it her bridegroom or a customer she anticipates? She is heavily draped and veiled, like a bride, but the dwarf servant who stands beside her smacks of the exotic and is more the sort of retainer to be expected in a house of questionable repute.

PORTRAITS IN CLAY

WOMEN WERE A FAVORITE SUBJECT of the craftsmen who made terra-cotta figurines from the 4th to the 1st centuries B.C. They are shown in their leisure moments, standing or sitting quietly, conversing, playing games, fanning themselves. These delicate little figurines have of-

57. YOUNG WOMEN WITH ELEGANT HAIRDOS (T 2442, T 3696)

ten been shattered into small fragments by the passing of the ages, but some of those fragments still provide vivid impressions of the women of Athens.

Earrings are never lacking on these elegant creatures, and they must have spent many hours on their elaborate hairdos (57). Some indicate by their clothing that they are engaged in religious duties (58). One is perhaps muffled

against the cold, but another pulls her mantle over her lower face in a gesture known from more complete figures of veiled dancers participating in an unknown rite (see 63). A third carries a ritual object on her head, supported by the heavy braids of her hair (see also 71). While not likenesses in any strict sense, these figurines help us imagine the women who were to be seen in and around the Agora.

58. WOMEN IN RELIGIOUS ROLES (T 8, T 1623, T 2111)

*We have offered here an overview of the lives of Athenian women, espe-
cially in the 5th and 4th centuries, a period when visual and textual evidence is particularly rich. In the epilogue that follows, we turn to a different Agora—the excavations of the 20th century—and to a different group
of women—the archaeologists who formed part of the excavation team of
the 1930s and later. These modern women crafted their own relationship to
the Agora as it reemerged from the soil of Athens, and it is their achieve-
ments on which we focus in the following pages.*

EPILOGUE:
WOMEN IN THE ATHENIAN AGORA (1931–)

THE AGORA EXCAVATIONS HAVE NEVER (yet) been directed by a woman,
but ever since the beginning women have run them; indeed, without
the efforts of women, the entire undertaking would have been doomed
to failure. Those profiled here joined the excavations in their youth and
went on to become outstanding figures in the field of classical archaeology. They were born in the early years of the 20th century to families
of wealth and position, but into a generation that expected women to
place obligations to family before personal ambition. The archaeological
careers of some were interrupted by periods of caretaking for children,
parents, and grandparents, making them pioneers in the challenging
task of balancing career and family obligations.

The American excavations in the Agora began on the 25th of May
1931, after long years of negotiation and planning. Lists of those who
participated in those early days show that women played a large part,
establishing a pattern that has continued to the present day (59). But
although in numbers women were almost the equal of men, their tasks
tended to be different. They were most frequently engaged in record-
keeping or in the study of "small finds"—terracotta figurines, coins,
pottery—while the men supervised the digging, did the architectural
drawings, and studied inscriptions and architecture. It is a familiar arrangement, though there were some notable exceptions, as we shall see.

59. THE AGORA STAFF IN 1933, THE THIRD YEAR OF EXCAVATION. VIRGINIA GRACE IS AT THE CENTER OF THE MIDDLE ROW; LUCY TALCOTT AND DOROTHY BURR [THOMPSON] ARE AT THE LEFT AND RIGHT ENDS OF THE FRONT ROW, RESPECTIVELY. DOROTHY'S FUTURE HUSBAND, HOMER THOMPSON, STANDS BEHIND HER. OTHER WOMEN PICTURED ARE JOSEPHINE SHEAR (IN THE FRONT ROW, BESIDE HER HUSBAND, THE DIRECTOR OF THE EXCAVATIONS); JOAN BUSH [VANDERPOOL], ELIZABETH DOW, AND GLADYS BAKER (MIDDLE ROW); AND MARY ZELIA PEASE [PHILIPPIDES] IN THE BACK ROW. THEIR RESPONSIBILITIES INCLUDED EXCAVATION, PHOTOGRAPHY, RECORD-KEEPING, AND STUDY OF THE COINS.

The small staff that conducted the first season in 1931 included three women: Josephine Shear (numismatist and wife of the director), Mary Wyckoff (artist), and Lucy Talcott (**60, 61**). Talcott, a blue-blooded New Englander, came to the excavations with a B.A. from Radcliffe ('21) and an M.A. from Columbia. Her assignment was to establish a system of record-keeping, not a glamorous task, but a critical one for the ultimate success of the project. Talcott had participated in fieldwork (including two brief stints of digging at the Agora in the early 1930s), but she found the process of documentation, curation, and study more to her taste, and she undertook her charge with energy and inspiration. She developed an elaborately cross-referenced recording system for finds and photographs, making it simple to move from any one aspect of the excavation to all the relevant data. She continued to oversee Agora records until 1958, and she guarded those documents fiercely; when an exasperated excavator inventoried an object as "another filthy stamped amphora handle," she descended on him like a ton of bricks, with the admonition, "Young man, this is a permanent record!" It was undoubtedly her firmness in situations like this that led some unknown Agora wit to dub the excavation a "despinocracy"—a state run by women (or, more precisely, by maiden ladies). Talcott

60. LUCY TALCOTT, PHOTO-GRAPHED BY ALISON FRANTZ ON ACROCORINTH (CA. 1939)

made a lasting contribution to scholarship in her publication (with collaborator Brian Sparkes) of the household pottery of the Archaic and

61. THE DESPINOCRAT ENTHRONED: LUCY TALCOTT AT WORK IN THE OLD EXCAVATION HEADQUARTERS (1937). THE SHELVES HOLD THE POTTERY THAT SHE LATER PUBLISHED WITH BRIAN SPARKES.

Classical periods, a work that has become a virtual bible for excavators, who are heavily dependent on pottery for the dating of strata and structures. She finished correcting the proofs only a week before her death in 1970.

The larger staff of the second field season (1932) included equal numbers of women and men. That year saw the entry onto the scene of two women who were to remain intimately involved with the Agora throughout their very long lives: Dorothy Burr (**62**) and Virginia Grace.

62. DOROTHY BURR [THOMPSON] ON HER FIRST EXCAVATION (PHLIUS, IN THE PELOPONNESE) IN 1924

Burr was the daughter of a Philadelphia lawyer and his novelist wife, both vigorous intellects who nurtured the scholarly development of their two daughters. Dorothy graduated from Bryn Mawr in 1923, won fellowships for two years of study in Greece, and continued on to graduate work, receiving her Ph.D. in 1931. The following year she began work at the excavations, the first woman to be appointed an Agora Fellow. Burr's research interests were stereotypically feminine—terracotta figurines—but, unlike Talcott, she had a passion for fieldwork, and her main responsibility at the Agora was to supervise excavation. Her field notebooks reveal a fine eye for detail and an almost obsessive drive to record everything as completely as possible—two excellent features in a field supervisor. How her career might otherwise have developed, we cannot know, but in 1934 she married fellow Agora Fellow Homer Thompson, who went on to become director of the Agora in 1946. From then on, her life was inextricably entwined with the excavations. With time out to bear and rear three daughters, she continued to supervise excavation into the 1950s and she was a regular presence in Athens and at the Agora thereafter, as she worked on the publication of the terracottas (**63**).

63. SOME OF THE FIGURINES DOROTHY THOMPSON STUDIED: (*clockwise from far left*) MANTLED DANCER, OLD MAN, TRAGIC ACTOR, THIEVING HEDGEHOG, 4TH TO 2ND CENTURIES B.C. (T 313, T 862, T 1731, T 3553)

Virginia Grace (**64**) studied the Classics at Brearley School, in her native New York, and then at Bryn Mawr, graduating in 1922. After some years spent teaching English and Mathematics in New York, she turned her attention again to the ancient world, and 1932 saw her joining the Agora records staff, while she worked towards the completion of her Ph.D., also at Bryn Mawr. She too did her share of fieldwork, though mostly at sites other than the Agora. Her life's work, however, was the study of transport amphoras (**65**), the commercial containers that the ancient Greeks used for the shipment of foodstuffs, primarily wine and oil. During her many years as an Agora Fellow, Grace built up an archive concerning these objects, which provide a wealth of information about the ancient economy, as well as serving as invaluable chronological markers. The amphoras, while pottery (a traditional feminine concern), frequently bear stamped inscriptions (traditionally a male preserve), and it was these inscriptions that Grace made her

64. VIRGINIA GRACE IN TURKEY DURING
THE SECOND WORLD WAR

65. TRANSPORT AMPHORA (SS 7582) AND DETAIL OF A STAMPED HANDLE (SS 7584)

particular focus, turning a largely neglected topic into a major field of inquiry. She soon grew to be an authority without peer in the study of the "SAH" (stamped amphora handle). From a small office in the Stoa of Attalos she corresponded with a network of excavators of all nationalities, whose first recourse when they found an amphora was to turn to Miss Grace (only the chosen few addressed her by her given name). She was still at her desk in the late 1980s, and at her death in 1994 she left behind an archive that continues be an important source of information on the ancient economy.

Alison Frantz (66) joined the Agora staff in 1934, initially as an assistant to Lucy Talcott in the Records Department. Although her first degree (from Smith in 1924) was in Classics, she turned to the Byzantine period in her graduate work at Columbia. She published a study of the 12th-century Church of the Holy Apostles, which still stands in the Agora today, and another on Late Antique Athens (3rd to 7th centuries), a span she referred to sardonically as "the grubby period." She was ahead of her time in insisting that the excavations should enlighten the whole history of Athens, not only its Classical golden age. Frantz is best known, however, for her archaeological photography. She later recalled how, at the age of five, she had watched her older brother working in the darkroom, and that "it gave the business a kind of glamour." In the early years of the excavation, the official position of Agora photographer was held by Herman Wagner, a member of the German Institute. He had other duties as well, however, and from 1935 onward, Frantz, reviving that early interest, undertook an increasing proportion of the photographic documentation of the excavations, finally achieving the title to go with her work when Wagner withdrew in 1939. She remained

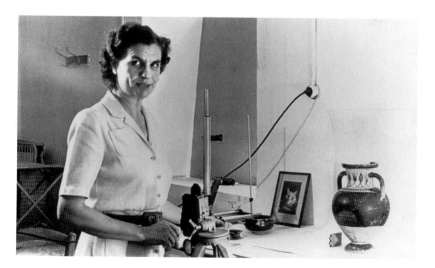

66. ALISON FRANTZ AT WORK (1947); NOTE PORTRAIT OF CAT.

67. HORSEMEN ON THE PARTHENON FRIEZE, PHOTOGRAPHED BY ALISON FRANTZ

photographer of the excavations until 1964, and her labors provide the primary visual record of 25 years of excavation, as well as of a series of Agora cats (another of her ardent enthusiasms). Her work was in high demand elsewhere as well; she made Greek sculpture her special focus, and her photographs of the Parthenon frieze (67) and of the sculptures of the Temple of Zeus at Olympia are classics. Although Frantz died in 1995, her work remains in demand, and archives of her negatives are maintained by the American School of Classical Studies and by Princeton University.

Margaret Crosby (68, 70; known to her friends as Missy, a nickname she traced back to being addressed as such by a friendly English boatman, encountered on a family holiday when she was eight years old) grew up in Minnesota. An active girlhood there left her with a taste and talent for hiking and mountaineering (she ultimately bagged most of Greece's major peaks). Like Virginia Grace, she was a member of the Bryn Mawr class of 1922. Two years of study in Europe followed before she began graduate work at Yale. There she concentrated on ancient history, but a season at the Yale expedition to Dura Europos, in Syria, deflected her decisively into archaeological fieldwork. Upon completion of her degree she joined the Agora excavations as an Agora Fellow and embarked on a life almost evenly divided between the archaeology of Athens, and family duties and pleasures back in the United States. Throughout her career, her work and interests crossed the unspoken gender lines. Her primary responsibility at the Agora was the supervision of fieldwork, and from 1935 to 1939, and then again from 1946 to 1955, she spent every season in the field (and field seasons in those days were epic in their duration—often as much as five months long). She also took on other duties (all the while continuing the daily excavation schedule), and oversaw the records operation in 1946, when Lucy Talcott was absent. In the realm of scholarship, it was the complex and highly technical fields of epigraphy (the study of inscriptions) and metrology

68. MISSY CROSBY IN THE 1930S

69. THE KIND OF PUZZLE MISSY CROSBY ENJOYED: AN INSCRIPTION RECORDING LEASES ON THE SILVER MINES AT LAUREION, LATER REUSED AS A DOOR SILL, 339/8 B.C. (I 2205)

70. MISSY CROSBY STUDYING ARCHITECTURAL FRAGMENTS IN THE BASEMENT OF THE AGORA MUSEUM (1956)

(weights and measures) that particularly attracted her—interests that drew on the same powerful linguistic talents she deployed as a code-breaker in the Office of Strategic Services during World War II. The inscription shown in **69**, which she published, is one of many found in the Agora that record leases on the famous silver mines of Athens, the material resource that formed the foundation of the rise of Athens in the 5th century B.C. and continued to fuel the economic power of Athens in later years. By the early 1960s Crosby had completed her excavation and publication assignments. By all accounts an unassuming and self-effacing woman, for all her scholarly abilities, she retired to a quiet life filled with travel, gardening, family, and friends. ❖

71. TERRACOTTA FIGURINE OF WOMAN CARRYING A WINNOWING BASKET WITH OFFERINGS OF FRUIT, CAKES, AND A WREATH, 4TH CENTURY B.C. (T 431)

MORE THAN TWO MILLENNIA separate the two groups of women we have encountered in these pages, and there is no denying that they lived very different lives. Nonetheless, there are some common themes. Both operated in a world where the rules were made by men; both were expected to— and most did—put duty to family ahead of other forms of personal fulfillment. Yet despite the challenges, both were very much forces to be reckoned with in their respective worlds, and in their different ways both made their mark as women in the Athenian Agora.

Credits

Except for Fig. 41, all color photography is the work of Craig Mauzy. Unless otherwise noted, black and white photographs are from the Archives of the Athenian Agora. Drawings (also from the Archives) are the work of John Travlos and William B. Dinsmoor Jr. (Fig. 1), Marian H. McAllister (Fig. 2), and William B. Dinsmoor Jr. (Figs. 18 and 30). Fig. 28 was painted by Piet de Jong. Other credits are as follows:

Fig. 3. © Martin von Wagner Museum, Würzburg.

Fig. 6. © Kunsthistorisches Museum, Bern.

Fig. 41. © 1999 The Metropolitan Museum of Art.

Fig. 60. Homer Thompson Papers, American School of Classical Studies at Athens.

Fig. 62. Courtesy of Pamela Sinkler-Todd.

Fig. 67. Alison Frantz Photographic Collection, American School of Classical Studies at Athens.

Fig. 68. Courtesy of Daniel Field.

Classical Authors Cited

p. 3, Xenophon, *Oikonomikos* 7.3 and 7.22

p. 8, Aristophanes, *Lysistrata*, 327–331

p. 15, Plutarch, *Table Talk*, 666–667

p. 19, Aristophanes, *Lysistrata*, 641–646

p. 22, Euripides, *Bacchai*, 874–876 (translation Arrowsmith)

p. 32, Aristophanes, *Lysistrata*, 574–586

p. 40, [Demosthenes] 59.122